Cyber Security

Essential principles to secure your organisation

Cyber Security

Essential principles to secure your organisation

ALAN CALDER

IT Governance Publishing

Every possible effort has been made to ensure that the information contained in this book is accurate at the time of going to press, and the publisher and the author cannot accept responsibility for any errors or omissions, however caused. Any opinions expressed in this book are those of the author, not the publisher. Websites identified are for reference only, not endorsement, and any website visits are at the reader's own risk. No responsibility for loss or damage occasioned to any person acting, or refraining from action, as a result of the material in this publication can be accepted by the publisher or the author.

Apart from any fair dealing for the purposes of research or private study, or criticism or review, as permitted under the Copyright, Designs and Patents Act 1988, this publication may only be reproduced, stored or transmitted, in any form, or by any means, with the prior permission in writing of the publisher or, in the case of reprographic reproduction, in accordance with the terms of licences issued by the Copyright Licensing Agency. Enquiries concerning reproduction outside those terms should be sent to the publisher at the following address:

IT Governance Publishing Ltd
Unit 3, Clive Court
Bartholomew's Walk
Cambridgeshire Business Park
Ely, Cambridgeshire
CB7 4EA
United Kingdom
www.itgovernancepublishing.co.uk

© Alan Calder 2020

The author has asserted the rights of the author under the Copyright, Designs and Patents Act, 1988, to be identified as the author of this work.

First published in the United Kingdom in 2020 by IT Governance Publishing.

ISBN 978-1-78778-209-9

ABOUT THE AUTHOR

Alan Calder is a leading author on IT governance and information security issues. He is Group CEO of GRC International Group plc, the AIM-listed company that owns IT Governance Ltd – the one-stop shop for books, tools, training and consultancy on governance, risk management and compliance.

Alan has written extensively on the issues of IT governance, information security and privacy. He is an international authority on ISO 27001, the international security standard, about which he wrote, with colleague Steve Watkins, the definitive compliance guide, *IT Governance – An International Guide to Data Security and ISO27001/ISO27002*. This work is based on his experience of leading the world's first successful implementation of BS 7799 (with the seventh edition published in 2019) and is the basis for the UK Open University's postgraduate course on information security.

Other books written by Alan include *The Case for ISO 27001 and Nine Steps to Success – An ISO 27001 Implementation Overview* (now in its third edition). He has also helped develop a wide range of information security management training courses that have been accredited by the International Board for IT Governance Qualifications (IBITGQ).

Alan is a frequent media commentator on information security and IT governance issues, and has contributed articles and expert comment to a wide range of trade, national and online news outlets.

He was previously CEO of Wide Learning, an e-learning supplier; of Focus Central London, a training and enterprise council; and of Business Link London City Partners, a government agency focused on helping growing businesses to develop.

CONTENTS

Introduction 1
Chapter 1: Information security and cyber security 3
  Laws, regulations and contracts 3
Chapter 2: Threats and vulnerabilities 5
  Technical threats 6
  Defending against malware 11
  Hacking 12
  Insecure configuration 15
Chapter 3: Security by design 19
  Example: TalkTalk data breach 21
Chapter 4: Human threats 23
  Social engineering 24
  Staying safe online 27
  Remote working 29
  Example: WannaCry 31
Chapter 5: Physical threats 35
  Defence in depth 37
  Physical security and mobile devices 38
  Example: KVM attacks 39
Chapter 6: Third-party threats 43
  Supply chain threats 43
  Example: Target data breach 49
Chapter 7: Securing the organisation 53
  Risk management 53
  Controls 55
Chapter 8: Incident response and management 59
  Continuity 60
Chapter 9: Standards and frameworks 63
  Taking the first steps 64
Chapter 10: Conclusion 67
Further reading 69

INTRODUCTION

The cyber security landscape is complex and constantly changing. Organisations large and small experience attacks every day, from simple phishing emails to intricate, detailed operations masterminded by criminal gangs, and for every vulnerability fixed, another pops up, ripe for exploitation.

Given the frequency of large-scale data breaches and cyber attacks in the news, you could be forgiven for thinking that it's impossible to defend your organisation against the predations of cyber attackers – after all, if massive multinationals can't stay secure, what hope is there for SMEs?

The answer is: more than you think. Cyber security doesn't have to cost vast amounts of money or take a short ice age to implement. No matter the size of your organisation, improving cyber security helps protect your data and that of your clients, improving business relations and opening the door to new opportunities.

This pocket guide will take you through the essentials of cyber security – the principles that underpin it, vulnerabilities and threats and the attackers who use them, and how to defend against them – so you can develop a cyber security programme for your organisation with confidence.

CHAPTER 1: INFORMATION SECURITY AND CYBER SECURITY

The terms 'information security' and 'cyber security' are often used interchangeably, when in fact they refer to different (albeit related) things.

Information security is concerned with ensuring the confidentiality, integrity and availability (C, I and A) of all information held by an organisation, irrespective of whether the information is electronic or in hard-copy format. As a result, information security generally involves considering physical and environmental controls alongside technological ones (lockable filing cabinets, key-code doors, etc.).

Cyber security is a subset of information security and is concerned with the same things, but where information security takes a generalist approach, cyber security focuses specifically on electronic information (including the physical aspects of defending that information). New cyber risks emerge almost daily, and the successful organisation must do all it can to stay ahead of the curve.

Laws, regulations and contracts

The days of cyber security as an afterthought are long past. Today's organisations collect, use and store more information than ever before, and the global regulatory system is beginning to catch up.

The introduction of the EU General Data Protection Regulation (GDPR) in 2018 marked a major milestone for data protection and privacy laws across the globe. Most of us remember the flood of 'we need your consent' emails that arrived in our inboxes in the days leading up to (and after) the GDPR took effect, but those emails were only the tip of the iceberg.

The GDPR places a wide range of security and privacy obligations on organisations that process EU residents' data and

1: Information security and cyber security

is supported by a regime of significant financial penalties (up to 4% of annual turnover or €20 million, whichever is greater). The Regulation also requires organisations based outside of the EU that process data on EU residents to appoint an EU representative, extending the reach of those obligations and penalties far beyond the EU's physical borders.

Another law that may be relevant is the Directive on security of network and information systems (NIS Directive). This places specific cyber security and business continuity obligations on digital service providers and operators of essential services such as power and water, with a view to mitigating the disruption that could occur as the result of a major cyber security incident.

While many organisations still grapple with the GDPR and NIS Directive, new laws such as the California Consumer Privacy Act (CCPA) or the Brazilian General Data Privacy Law (Lei Geral de Proteção de Dados Pessoais) are being introduced around the world, and further legislation is expected in the coming years. The increasing regulatory focus on data protection, privacy and continuity of key services inevitably leads to a greater focus on cyber security, as so much of the information held by organisations is in electronic formats, and the majority of essential services rely on electronic infrastructure.

It's not just laws that mandate effective cyber security. Cyber security obligations in contracts are increasingly common, as organisations begin to recognise the risks posed by information sharing between suppliers and partners. If your organisation takes card payments, for example, banks will expect you to adhere to the requirements of the Payment Card Industry Data Security Standard (PCI DSS), while many government contracts mandate a minimum level of cyber security to enter the tendering process.

CHAPTER 2: THREATS AND VULNERABILITIES

Risk is an inevitable part of life. Every time you do something in which the outcome is uncertain, you take a risk, whether it's something simple like crossing the road, or something complex like undergoing surgery. Risk is a function of uncertainty – without uncertainty, there is no risk.

Different business fields approach risk in different ways, but the general principles remain the same: the likelihood of an adverse event is mapped against the effect that event would have were it to occur. If the outcome is severe and the likelihood high enough, then it is sensible to take steps to protect against it – usually by reducing the damage caused by the outcome, or by reducing the likelihood that it will occur in the first place.

Cyber security risk derives from a combination of threats and vulnerabilities: vulnerabilities are exploited by threats to achieve certain goals, such as accessing a secure network or installing malware. This does not mean that cyber security risk is limited to deliberate actions by malicious actors – a leaky roof of a server room (vulnerability) can be 'exploited' by a rainstorm (threat), with potentially catastrophic results.

Threats and vulnerabilities can take many forms. A database that fails to properly sanitise user inputs, for instance, might be exploited by an attacker using an SQL injection to gain access to sensitive data, while unpatched software might allow an attacker to install malware, with any number of nasty results – wiping files or holding them to ransom, to name just two.

Software and hardware are always evolving, and the same is true for vulnerabilities – each advance brings new security challenges. Even longstanding, trusted software or hardware is not immune. In 2018, major computer chip manufacturers were stunned to discover that their processors had major security flaws (named 'Meltdown' and 'Spectre') at the hardware level

2: Threats and vulnerabilities

since 1995 – processors that are believed to be in almost every modern computer across the globe.[1]

Cyber threat actors come in all shapes and sizes too. While our first thought may be of the 'nerd' locked in a bedroom writing code for a prank, the reality is very different. Organised crime gangs, 'hacktivists' pushing a political agenda, and even state-supported actors all represent potential threats, irrespective of the size of your organisation.

Perhaps the most pervasive threat actor is something you can't live without – your employees. Even discounting 'insider threats' (the term used to describe employees who are actively looking to harm their organisation in some way, often because they are unhappy), many cyber security incidents are caused inadvertently by employees who lack awareness of the risks. According to a report by Verizon, 34% of data breaches in 2019 involved internal actors.[2]

Technical threats

When we think about cyber security, technical threats are usually the first thing that comes to mind. The news abounds with stories of vast data breaches that are eventually traced to some obscure vulnerability in hardware or software, and phishing emails carrying malware drop into millions of inboxes every day, all over the world. Every inch of progress towards security is a hard-fought battle, and to fight effectively, you need to understand the enemy's weapons.

---

[1] Samuel Gibbs, "Meltdown and Spectre: 'worst ever' CPU bugs affect virtually all computers", The Guardian, January 2018, *https://www.theguardian.com/technology/2018/jan/04/meltdown-spectre-worst-cpu-bugs-ever-found-affect-computers-intel-processors-security-flaw*.

[2] Verizon, "Verizon 2019 Data Breach Investigations Report (DBIR)" *https://enterprise.verizon.com/en-gb/resources/reports/dbir/2019/summary-of-findings/*.

2: Threats and vulnerabilities

Malware

Malware has existed in one form or another since computers became commonplace. Self-replicating software was conceived in the 1940s, and one of the first viruses, known as Creeper, was created in the early 1970s, infecting US government computers and displaying "I'm the Creeper, catch me if you can" on the screen.

Since then, there has been an explosion of malware. Sites on the dark web offer a vast array of malware programs for sale, and new malware appears daily, taking advantage of the latest vulnerabilities in a never-ending arms race between the malicious actors who craft it and the cyber security professionals who defend against it. 'Malware' as a category encompasses a range of malicious programs, each of which operates differently.

Virus

Viruses are self-replicating programs designed to spread from computer to computer and deliver a payload. Viruses are not standalone programs – they are bits of code that need to be hidden in other programs to function and replicate. When the user runs the 'host' program, the virus infects the system and does its work.

Once it has infected a system, the virus has two goals: replicate itself as much as possible and deliver the payload – ideally without being spotted. Some of the earliest viruses were called 'boot sector' viruses, because they infected sections of a drive that are read when a computer is booted up, making them hard to detect, and were often spread through the sharing of floppy discs (which were still in common use at the time).

Some of the most common viruses of the Internet era are macro viruses – viruses written in the scripting language found in Microsoft® Office and embedded in Office files, such as Excel spreadsheets or Word documents. Opening the document allows the virus to infect the system, with potentially catastrophic results. Emails featuring infected Office documents have been a common attack vector since the early 1990s, so much so that

2: Threats and vulnerabilities

'don't open suspicious attachments' has become a cyber security maxim.

Worms

If the principal characteristic of a virus is that it is a self-replicating program that must be embedded in another program to function, then a worm is a virus with that limitation removed. Worms do not need to be embedded in other programs and can replicate without user interaction, making them especially dangerous.

One of the best-known worms in recent years is Stuxnet. Discovered in 2010, this highly complex worm targeted industrial control systems in an Iranian nuclear facility, changing the speed of uranium enrichment centrifuges until a large number broke from the strain. Commonly believed to have been developed by US and Israel intelligence agencies, Stuxnet is considered by some the world's first "cyber-weapon of geopolitical significance".[3]

Ransomware

Ransomware exploded into the public consciousness with the WannaCry attack on the NHS in 2017, which affected up to 70,000 devices including hospital equipment.[4] Other major organisations such as FedEx and Renault were also affected, along with a number of universities and government institutions across the globe.

---

[3] Holger Stark, "Stuxnet Virus Opens New Era of Cyber War", Der Spiegel, August 2011,
https://www.spiegel.de/international/world/mossad-s-miracle-weapon-stuxnet-virus-opens-new-era-of-cyber-war-a-778912.html.

[4] Robert Mendick, "Cyber attack on NHS would trigger full Nato response, says alliance's general secretary", The Telegraph, August 2019, *https://www.telegraph.co.uk/news/2019/08/27/cyber-attack-nhs-would-trigger-full-nato-response-says-alliances/*.

2: Threats and vulnerabilities

Ransomware is a payload, usually transmitted by self-replicating worms or Trojans, that encrypts or otherwise prevents access to the user's files until a ransom is paid (usually in Bitcoin). Some ransomware will take a copy of the user's files and threaten to publish them, but the effect is the same – pay up or lose out.

Before the 2017 WannaCry attacks (which occurred worldwide, not just in the UK), ransomware primarily targeted individual consumers. The 2017 attacks marked the beginning of a shift in focus, with 81% of ransomware attacks in 2018 targeting organisations, not consumers.[5]

Trojan horses

Trojan horses, or just 'Trojans', are a type of malware that pretend to be something else. The name comes from the ancient Greek story about the fall of Troy.

Trojans generally masquerade as legitimate programs to trick you into activating them, though some can spread on their own without user interaction. One of the most common attack vectors is email, as Trojans can be embedded in seemingly innocuous attachments such as spreadsheets or Word files. Once activated, the Trojan sends spoof emails to everyone in the address book, further spreading the infection.

Trojans can carry almost any kind of payload, but keyloggers and 'backdoors' that allow access to sensitive information or systems are common. Trojans that contain keyloggers or other methods of capturing information usually send the information to a master server from time to time; these transmissions can sometimes be the only way to identify that a Trojan is present.

---

[5] Symantec, "Internet Security Threat Report", Volume 24, February 2019, *https://www.symantec.com/content/dam/symantec/docs/reports/istr-24-2019-en.pdf*.

2: Threats and vulnerabilities

Hybrid malware

Hybrid malware is malware that combines different aspects of other malware in order to be more effective.

Most of the malware we encounter today is a hybrid – for example, a worm with a ransomware payload, like WannaCry. Worms with Trojan or rootkit payloads are responsible for most 'botnets' – connected groups of computers or other Internet-enabled devices that are used to conduct distributed denial-of-service (DDoS) attacks, where a large number of devices communicate with the target simultaneously to overload it. Internet of Things (IoT) devices are particularly prone to botnet infections and related threats because they tend to have less effective security at both hardware and software levels (though this is beginning to change as awareness of IoT threats increases).

'Living off the land' and 'fileless' malware

A relatively recent development in the cyber threat landscape, 'living off the land' attacks involve the use of legitimate system and administrative tools (such as PowerShell or TeamViewer) that are already installed on the target system. These attacks can be difficult to detect, as the malicious activity blends in with other, legitimate administrative use of such tools.

A related concept is 'fileless' malware. Living off the land techniques are sometimes called fileless malware as they only involve existing, legitimate software and don't require, for example, the user to download an infected file. This isn't entirely accurate. Instead, fileless malware is better thought of as an attack that does not require or generate additional files that antivirus or anti-malware software might identify as suspicious. Examples include malware that runs and delivers its payload entirely within system memory, scripts embedded in the Windows registry system, and some browser-based cryptojacking attacks.

2: Threats and vulnerabilities

Defending against malware

Raise awareness

If employees don't understand cyber security and the role they play in protecting the organisation, even the best technical defences won't help. Training and awareness help employees recognise threats and take appropriate action.

Keep systems up to date

Software and hardware updates often include fixes for known vulnerabilities and should be applied promptly (e.g. through a patch management system) when they are made available by the vendor. Systems that are no longer supported by the vendor are a common factor in many data breaches and should be replaced or retired.

Deploy anti-malware tools

Antivirus and anti-malware software, firewalls and similar tools all help protect against malware. These programs should always be kept up to date to help protect against newly discovered vulnerabilities.

Secure backups

Taking regular backups has long been cyber security best practice, and backups are one of the best defences against ransomware – no need to pay a ransom if you can restore your files with a few clicks.[6] Some emerging strains of ransomware

---

[6] This is something of a simplification. While effective backups make it possible to recover from ransomware and similar attacks, that doesn't mean you should rely on the backups as the only means of defence. Malware (especially ransomware) can be difficult to remove, and the process of restoring your data from backups is necessarily time consuming, even for small organisations. It is far better to prevent the attack from occurring in the first place.

2: Threats and vulnerabilities

can infect or delete backups, however, making it more important than ever to ensure that any backup service has adequate information security measures, including antivirus and anti-malware tools.[7] Malware can remain dormant for long periods before triggering, so it is also important that backups are run frequently and retained for long enough to allow recovery in such an event.

Hacking

At the most basic level, criminal hackers find and exploit flaws and vulnerabilities in hardware and software. There is no shortage of flaws to find, either – no piece of software or hardware is truly immune, and new vulnerabilities are identified every day. Zero-day vulnerabilities (a vulnerability in newly released software or hardware that the manufacturer is not aware of) are a favourite target of criminal hackers, as attacks are more likely to be successful.

Criminal hackers are a disparate group encompassing everything from the stereotypical basement-dwelling nerd to state-supported 'hacker teams' with extensive financial backing and equipment. To better classify the threat posed by each type of criminal hacker, they are usually categorised as follows:

Script kiddie

This term refers to low-skilled, often young criminal hackers who use prebuilt tools to carry out low-sophistication attacks, usually without any real understanding of the underlying principles. While this doesn't make them any less threatening – the tools they use are built by skilled criminal hackers who know exactly what they're doing – it does mean that the vulnerabilities they exploit are usually common ones for which fixes may

---

[7] Lawrence Abrams, "Zenis Ransomware Encrypts Your Data & Deletes Your Backups", Bleeping Computer, March 2018, *https://www.bleepingcomputer.com/news/security/zenis-ransomware-encrypts-your-data-and-deletes-your-backups/*.

2: Threats and vulnerabilities

already be available, and against which basic cyber security measures offer protection.

A notable proportion of cyber crime occurs in exactly this way – inexperienced malicious actors purchasing simple tools or botnets to carry out low-level attacks that, despite their simplicity, still present a tenable threat to the organisation. Many attackers have little or no appreciation of the wider effects of their attacks or the principles that underpin them, in part because it is so easy to buy hacking tools and malware kits online. They have little concept of the real effect or cost of their attacks and will often claim that the attack was only done 'for the lols'.

Blackhats

Skilled criminal hackers who identify new vulnerabilities and develop the tools used to exploit them are known as 'blackhats'. Financial motivation is common – many blackhats sell the hacking tools they develop through online black markets, though they may also carry out attacks themselves in the hope of extorting payment (e.g. via ransomware) or selling stolen information to other criminals.

Unlike script kiddies, blackhats know exactly what they're doing and usually have a clear idea of what they want to achieve, making them some of the most effective and feared attackers.

Hacktivists

Hacktivist is more a classification of motivation than of skill or ability. Hacktivists carry out attacks to promote an agenda, though the ideology is often ill-defined and may vary over time. Hacktivist attacks are difficult to predict, not only due to the disparate nature of the groups themselves but also because of the wide range of potential targets. Notorious hacktivist group Anonymous, for example, has conducted attacks on the Church

2: Threats and vulnerabilities

of Scientology, Sony Online Entertainment, Islamic State and Donald Trump, to name but a few.[8]

State actors and cyber warfare

Cyber warfare may seem like something out of a science-fiction novel, but cyber attacks carried out by nation-state actors are increasingly common. In July 2019, Microsoft reported that it had notified almost 10,000 customers (84% of which were enterprise accounts) that they had been "targeted or compromised by nation-state attacks" over the course of the previous year.[9]

State-sponsored attackers often have access to extensive funding and equipment, and may operate with actual or tacit legal immunity in their country, making them very difficult to bring to justice. Nation-state attacks also tend to be highly targeted and focused on achieving specific goals, such as exfiltrating intellectual property or disrupting critical infrastructure. The 2010 Stuxnet attack on Iranian nuclear facilities (mentioned earlier in this book) is an infamous example of cyber warfare.

Ethical hacking

Not every hacker is a cyber criminal. Ethical hackers use the same tools and techniques as criminal hackers to search for vulnerabilities, but instead of exploiting them, they inform the system operator so that the vulnerabilities can be fixed. This approach, known as 'penetration testing', helps organisations

---

[8] Brian Feldman, "An Incomplete List of Every Person, Place, and Institution Upon Which Anonymous Has 'Declared War'", New York Magazine, March 2016, *http://nymag.com/intelligencer/2016/03/everything-upon-which-anonymous-has-declared-war.html*.

[9] Tom Burt, "New cyberthreats require new ways to protect democracy", July 2019, *https://blogs.microsoft.com/on-the-issues/2019/07/17/new-cyberthreats-require-new-ways-to-protect-democracy/*.

2: Threats and vulnerabilities

identify and resolve vulnerabilities before they fall victim to an attack.

There are several types of penetration test. Two of the most common are external vulnerability scans, which highlight weak spots in how you connect to the Internet and other external systems, and internal vulnerability scans, which pinpoint weaknesses in internal networks that could be exploited by malicious insiders or external attackers who have managed to access them. Other types include web application penetration tests and wireless network penetration tests, which look for weaknesses in web applications or in your wireless networks; phishing simulations; and even physical entry tests that highlight weaknesses in the boundary of your premises that might allow an attacker to enter (e.g. via a social engineering attack).

Legitimate ethical hackers hold an internationally recognised certification and are subject to a strict code of conduct. The scope of testing is agreed with the client, ensuring no disruption to operational systems and services. Penetration testing services are used by organisations of all sizes, but are particularly useful for small and medium-sized organisations that do not have the in-house expertise to carry out such testing themselves.

Information security standards and frameworks, such as ISO/IEC 27001:2013 or the UK's Cyber Essentials scheme (among others), strongly encourage the use of penetration testing to highlight vulnerabilities for remediation.

Insecure configuration

Many technical threats rely on or take advantage of poorly configured devices to do their dirty work. Software and hardware are usually supplied in their default state, with preinstalled applications, default passwords and the like. This makes life easier for consumers, but it also creates risk for your organisation.

Preinstalled software is common on desktop and mobile devices, but each item of software presents its own risks. Default accounts and passwords, insecure transmission protocols, unexpected open ports and worse can arise simply because it's

2: Threats and vulnerabilities

the software's default setting. The same is true of more technical hardware, such as routers or server equipment. An attacker can purchase a list of default passwords for a particular device, and software that scans the Internet for those devices, then carry out attacks once a suitable device is found.

Preinstalled administrative tools pose a major risk, as they allow the user much more control than consumer-focused applications and can potentially enable more damaging attacks. Network and server configurations should also be a primary concern, as misconfiguration can be the gateway through which an attacker gains access to sensitive areas or information.

Applications for mobile devices often require permissions that are not strictly necessary to perform the task at hand, like access to microphones or cameras. Mobile devices often don't have antivirus or anti-malware protection installed either, making them especially vulnerable. Risks also arise if your organisation allows the use of personal devices to access secure networks or files, or allows users to freely install software.

It is far easier to begin from a state of secure configuration than to apply one retrospectively. The first thing to do is to take an inventory of all hardware and software so you know what you're dealing with. Once you've done this, you can develop secure baseline configurations that define the permitted software, hardware and necessary security-hardening steps to ensure security. Those steps might include changing all default passwords, limiting administrative tools to authorised, secure administrative accounts, disabling default accounts, or removing unnecessary software or peripherals. Your baseline should also include antivirus and anti-malware software as standard on all systems, including mobile devices.

You should also configure servers and networks with intrusion detection software so you can monitor suspected attacks. Instead of having one big network that everything connects to, segment it to make it harder for unauthorised users to access sensitive data or systems (especially where the network connects to payment systems such as point-of-sale devices, etc.). Network, server and database access channels should employ brute-force

2: Threats and vulnerabilities

password protection (where login is disabled for a time after a set number of failed attempts) to defend against bulk password attacks.

One common configuration issue is inadvertent information disclosure, where HTTP headers and standard system responses provide information that would be useful to attackers, such as software names, version numbers and other information that a malicious actor could use to craft more effective attacks. Protect against this by disabling or modifying HTTP response headers and system responses so they do not disclose identifiers.

Password reset functions are another area in which information disclosure is common. If your password reset function confirms whether the login information entered is in use or not in use (e.g. 'this username is not recognised'), then it is possible for an attacker to enumerate a list of usernames that could later be used to attack the system. To prevent this, configure password reset functions to return a generic message (e.g. 'if you are a registered user, a password reset email will be sent') regardless of whether a recognised or unrecognised username is entered.

Once you have defined your baseline configurations, implement controls that prevent users installing their own software or making other potentially harmful changes. Develop a patch management policy that ensures patches and updates are applied promptly (e.g. within two weeks of release), and a change management procedure so that any future changes to the baseline configuration are assessed for risk and suitability before they are implemented.

Once you have defined and rolled out your configurations, consider using periodic vulnerability scans to identify any weak spots you might have missed. Even the most comprehensive baseline configuration may still contain weaknesses, and new vulnerabilities arise daily – it's better to stay ahead of the game than to learn the hard way.

CHAPTER 3: SECURITY BY DESIGN

For a product (whether software or hardware) to be secure, it must be developed with security in mind from the outset. This was a challenge in the days when most development still used the 'waterfall' model; in the era of Agile and similar, more iterative methodologies, the challenge has never been greater.

Secure development is not a new concept. The rapid spread of computers and the Internet in the late 1990s highlighted the myriad security flaws and issues in the era's operating systems, software and hardware. Viruses and worms proliferated, and customers demanded action. At Microsoft, Bill Gates's famous 2002 'Trustworthy computing' memo outlined the need for security to become an intrinsic aspect of computing, such that Microsoft products would be seen to be as safe and reliable as the water or electricity supply.[10]

As a result, Microsoft developed the Security Development Lifecycle (SDL).[11] Adopted by Microsoft in 2004 and applicable to third-party developers as well as Microsoft's own, the SDL laid the foundation for secure development methodologies. In 2008, Microsoft made information on the SDL available free of charge, and it was quickly adopted and adapted by a wide range of industries.

Secure development methodologies are now well established, yet far too many organisations still consider security something that can be 'bolted on' late in the development process. Such an

---

[10] Bill Gates, "Bill Gates: Trustworthy Computing", Wired, January 2002, *https://www.wired.com/2002/01/bill-gates-trustworthy-computing/*.

[11] Microsoft Security Development Lifecycle, Microsoft, accessed October 2019, *https://www.microsoft.com/en-us/securityengineering/sdl*.

3: Security by design

approach is expensive and time-consuming – especially where it requires code to be reworked and tested – and is rarely as effective as accounting for security holistically throughout the development lifecycle.

Consider two common cyber attacks: SQL injection and cross-site scripting (XSS). Both can have major consequences (see the iconic *XKCD* strip "Exploits of a Mom" for one example[12]), and the vulnerabilities that permit the attacks are easily identified and exploited by readily available, automated tools – yet both attacks can be easily prevented if secure development principles are applied.

Secure development methodologies vary from organisation to organisation, but the core principles generally remain the same:

Knowledge and training

Developers should be trained to understand and apply security techniques during development. Keeping this knowledge up to date is perhaps the biggest challenge, as new vulnerabilities are identified every day, so regular refresher courses and familiarity with the rapidly moving cyber security landscape are critical.

Identify security requirements

To prevent clashes and no-win decisions later in the development cycle, it's important to identify security requirements as part of the same process that identifies customer and stakeholder requirements, and to review them frequently as the project progresses. Remember that cyber security begins with three core requirements that should always be accounted for: confidentiality, integrity and availability (sometimes called the 'CIA triad').

---

[12] Randall Munroe, "Exploits of a Mom", *XKCD*, accessed October 2019, *https://xkcd.com/327/*.

3: Security by design

Identify design security risks

Now you know what the design is expected to achieve, you can identify and assess the risks posed by each feature and take steps to mitigate them. Development is an evolving process, so the risk assessment should be repeated periodically to make sure no new issues have crept in, and that all existing ones have been adequately resolved.

Risk assess components

Products, whether software or hardware, often incorporate third-party components. Such components save time and money, but they bring their own risks. Those risks need to be identified and mitigated before the component is incorporated.

Mitigating risks associated with third-party components is often difficult, because you have no control over the third party's development processes. Cultivating good relationships with suppliers can go some way to dealing with this issue, but sometimes the only way to be sure is to perform security tests on the component yourself.

Perform security testing throughout the development lifecycle

Security testing should be performed regularly throughout the development lifecycle to ensure that security vulnerabilities introduced during development are identified and resolved. Organisations that don't have in-house expertise should consider engaging a penetration testing provider at an appropriate stage of the process.

Example: TalkTalk data breach

In 2015, TalkTalk was hit by an SQL injection attack that exposed the personal data of more than 150,000 customers, for which the Information Commissioner's Office (ICO) proposed a fine of £400,000 (later settled under agreement for £320,000).

The ICO's report noted multiple cyber security failings alongside the SQL injection vulnerability, including two previous SQL injection attacks on the same web pages that went

3: Security by design

unnoticed due to a lack of monitoring. To make matters worse, the exposed customer information was stored in an outdated legacy database that lacked a security fix made available by the vendor more than three years earlier (which would have prevented the attack, had it been applied).[13]

Code injection attacks have been a known, recurring vulnerability for more than 20 years, and any effective secure development process would have highlighted this fact and therefore prevented this problem from ever occurring. The same is true for the legacy database – an effective process would have highlighted the risks associated with unsupported software, especially when connected to the Internet, and mandated that the database be ported to a more recent or alternative version.

If that proved impossible, it would have at least ensured that the security patch made available by the vendor three years prior was installed. Instead, the site went live and TalkTalk's customers lost out.

---

[13] Alex Hern, "TalkTalk hit with record £400k fine over cyber-attack", The Guardian, October 2016, *https://www.theguardian.com/business/2016/oct/05/talktalk-hit-with-record-400k-fine-over-cyber-attack*.

CHAPTER 4: HUMAN THREATS

Some of the biggest threats to cyber security come not from technology, but from the people who use it. According to a 2019 report by Verizon, 34% of security incidents (out of 41,686 analysed) were attributable to internal actors.[14]

Most insider threats are not actively or deliberately malicious. In fact, most of the time, cyber incidents that are traced to insiders are simple mistakes that anyone could make, like being tricked by a cloned email. A 2018 report by Ponemon Institute that surveyed more than 3,000 insider incidents attributed only 23% of them to criminal and malicious insiders.[15]

Protecting against human threats requires training: employees need to know how to identify and respond to phishing emails and other commonly encountered threats. They also need to know how to go about their daily job in a secure manner, whether that be locking filing cabinets when not in use, or knowing which databases contain sensitive information and how to access them securely. Secure working doesn't just protect the organisation from attacks, but also helps prevent accidental damage to information and information systems by promoting a conscientious approach to daily tasks.

Training is a good defence against attacks that take advantage of human nature, but it is equally important to develop a culture of security within the organisation, and an environment that supports it. Employees who are busy or stressed are less likely to remember and apply the training, and more likely to fall victim to common attacks.

---

[14] Verizon, "2019 Data Breach Investigations Report", August 2019, *https://enterprise.verizon.com/en-gb/resources/reports/dbir/*.

[15] Ponemon Institute and ObserveIT, "2018 Cost of Insider Threats: Global Organizations", April 2018, *https://www.ponemon.org/blog/tag/cost%20of%20insider%20threats*.

4: Human threats

Employees who fear punishment for falling victim to an attack will be less likely to report suspected attacks, which puts your whole organisation at risk. The culture of security you create, and the environment in which that culture operates, must be positive. The blame game doesn't help anyone.

Social engineering

Social engineering attacks have existed since the early days of human civilisation. From the ancient Greeks' use of the Trojan Horse to attack Troy, to Victor Lustig's efforts in the 1920s to sell the Eiffel Tower for scrap (twice), con artists have plied their trade and caused misery to millions.

Social engineering is a type of attack in which a person is manipulated into doing something they shouldn't, such as opening an infected email attachment or divulging sensitive information. Social engineering attacks are one of the most common cyber security concerns, with 83% of respondents to Proofpoint's 2019 "State of the Phish" report experiencing phishing attacks in 2018.[16]

Social engineering attacks come in all shapes and sizes, from the 'classic' email attachment scam to complex 'pretextual' attacks in which the attacker manufactures a convincing scenario to achieve their goal.

Phishing

The most prevalent form of social engineering attack, phishing is the act of fraudulently obtaining information through electronic communications that appear to be from legitimate sources. Phishing comes in a variety of flavours depending on the target and the method of execution, but the most common vector is email.

---

[16] Proofpoint, "State of the Phish 2019 Report", January 2019, *https://www.proofpoint.com/us/corporate-blog/post/2019-state-phish-report-attack-rates-rise-account-compromise-soars*.

4: Human threats

Phishing emails have come a long way since the infamous 'Nigerian Prince' emails of the early 2000s. While some phishing emails still feature poor spelling and grammar and describe implausible scenarios that demand the urgent provision of your bank details, many are now far more subtle.

Most phishing emails are crafted to look just like an email from a legitimate sender – using the same fonts, logos and phrasing to convince you that the email is real, and using spoofed sender addresses to further enhance their legitimate appearance. The email will invariably ask you to open an attachment or click a link – perhaps to reset your password, or to update your payment information. Do so, and you become the victim.

Links in phishing emails will appear to be legitimate, but closer examination often highlights discrepancies like deliberate misspelling or use of dubious subdomains. The website you visit may have been created to steal your credentials, or the attachment you open may contain a malware payload that gives the attacker access to your network. The outcome is rarely immediately visible, as in most cases this would trigger a security response.

While a large percentage of phishing is untargeted 'bulk' attacks, more targeted methods are also used. Phishing that targets specific organisations or persons is called 'spear phishing', and often masquerades as emails from suppliers or other trusted third parties. A further variant is 'whaling', which targets senior executives with well-crafted emails designed to appeal to them specifically – perhaps masquerading as a contract dispute or escalated customer complaint. The flipside of whaling is business email compromise (BEC), in which the phishing email appears to come from a senior executive.

Other variants of phishing include phishing by phone or voice over Internet Protocol ('vishing') and by text message ('smishing'). A determined attacker can compromise any communication medium to deliver phishing attacks with enough effort.

The payload delivered depends on the type of attack. Untargeted phishing emails generally deliver malware (e.g. a worm or a

4: Human threats

Trojan), while whaling and BEC attacks often attempt to steal login credentials or extort payment.

Social media

Social media may be a great tool for communicating and sharing information, but like any online activity, it comes with its own set of risks. We happily share our photos, locations and sensitive information with little thought to our own security or privacy. We also rarely consider the risks our social media activity might pose to others – whether friends, family or the organisations we work for.

When sharing information on social media, it is important to consider how that information might be used. Password reset functions, for example, often have a security question as an additional layer of security: your mother's maiden name, your first pet, or a school you attended. You may think your answer is something that few people would know, but if you've posted family details or photos of pets on social media, or signed up to a school reunion page, then that information might be freely available to criminal hackers.

Information shared on social media is of immense value, but passive information collection isn't the only risk. 'Catfishing' – the use of a fake profile to elicit sensitive information from a person – is common on social media platforms, including dating apps and websites. The fake profile will begin an apparently innocuous conversation to gain the recipient's trust, then over time, will manipulate the recipient into providing more information.

Catfishing is frequently used to perform reconnaissance on an organisation, eliciting information from the organisation's employees in preparation for an attack. It is also used to steal credentials, or even whole identities.

Social media apps can also be a source of risk, even when developed by large organisations like Facebook. In 2018, security researchers identified a vulnerability in Facebook's

4: Human threats

Messenger app that allowed criminal hackers to expose a user's contact list and messages.[17]

To defend against social media attacks, develop a policy on the use of social media on work computers. It should prohibit employees from posting sensitive information about your organisation on social media and might also ban installing social media apps on mobiles and other portable devices. Train employees to understand the risks posed by social media to help them stay safe at home as well as at work.

Staying safe online

Using the Internet has been an everyday experience for so long that most of us give it little thought. We visit our favourite websites and go about our business online without much consideration for the risks, yet the simple act of browsing to a website can expose us to malware or other threats. While it is impossible to remove the risks entirely, safe browsing principles go a long way towards mitigating them.

Keep tools up to date, and use them

Your organisation's policies should ensure that browser and security tools (like antivirus or anti-malware software) are up to date and switched on. This ensures your systems always have the latest available security fixes. Policies should also take advantage of browser-based protection (e.g. warnings when a potentially unsafe website is visited) where available.

Browser-based protection should not be confused with the 'Do Not Track' (DNT) functionality common to most major browsers, which sends a message to the website or application asking it not to track the session. Supporting DNT requests is entirely voluntary on the part of the website or app operator, so

---

[17] Shannon Liao, "Facebook Messenger had a vulnerability that could let hackers see who you contact", The Verge, March 2019, *https://www.theverge.com/2019/3/7/18254788/facebook-messenger-vulnerability-attack-imperva-iframe-malicious*.

4: Human threats

very few websites honour them, making DNT essentially useless.

The W3C Tracking Protection Working Group, who were responsible for development of the DNT specification, closed in early 2019 citing lack of adoption. Apple removed the functionality from its browsers shortly afterwards over concerns that it could contribute to browser 'fingerprinting'.[18] While DNT is only one datapoint among many that could be used to identify a given browser, this is perhaps the only browser security tool that should be switched off.

Check for secure connections and legitimate website addresses

Train users to check URLs carefully before entering login credentials or other sensitive information and never input any sensitive information into an unsecured website. Users should check to see if the website uses HTTPS and has a valid SSL certificate (by looking for the padlock icon next to the address bar) before entering any login details – the certificate should have the same name as the company whose website they are trying to access.

It is important that users understand that the padlock icon alone doesn't mean the site is safe – it only means that the information between the browser and the website is encrypted and cannot be read if intercepted. Attackers can spoof the entire address bar, including the padlock (especially on mobile devices where screen space is a limited commodity), or register a legitimate SSL certificate for a domain name containing international characters that superficially resembles a legitimate site.

Some browsers will display a warning when clicking a link that contains international characters, and if you ignore the warning and navigate to the site itself, will display the international

---

[18] Glenn Fleishman, "How the tragic death of Do Not Track ruined the web for everyone", Fast Company, March 2019, *https://www.fastcompany.com/90308068/how-the-tragic-death-of-do-not-track-ruined-the-web-for-everyone*.

4: Human threats

character in a web-friendly variant of the Unicode format (so the 'i' in the spoofed link above displays as XN—rog). This at least shows the user that the address uses international characters (assuming of course that the address bar hasn't been spoofed as well), but finding this out while using the site is hardly ideal.

Handle with care

Train users to be careful what they click. Before clicking any link, whether on a website or in an email, users can mouseover it to see the destination URL. If it doesn't match the visible link, or the destination URL looks suspicious, users should understand not to click it.

Remote working

The freedom to work from home, on the train, or in another country entirely is a huge boon to employees and employers, but it brings with it a host of risks. Controlling those risks is necessarily harder because remote employees operate outside your organisation's logical perimeter (the boundary within which your networks and information reside). Extending those boundaries without effective controls makes your security more permeable than it would otherwise be.

Of all the risks associated with remote working, loss or theft is probably the most common. Mobile devices such as phones or laptops are easily lost or forgotten while travelling, and theft has long been a risk for portable equipment of any kind. Your remote working policy should contain requirements for the handling of mobile devices while off-premises: don't leave devices unattended, especially in public places; don't store devices in vehicles, especially overnight; don't leave devices unlocked, etc.

Remote working invariably requires the worker to connect to the Internet. Free Wi-Fi is available in a wide range of places, from trains to cafés, but using it can be risky. Criminal hackers can create false wireless access points to harvest credentials and other sensitive network traffic, while poorly secured networks can expose you to malware or man-in-the-middle (MITM) attacks.

4: Human threats

The safest option is to prohibit such devices from connecting to public Wi-Fi at all, but this isn't always possible. If use of a public Wi-Fi network can't be avoided, the next best option is to connect to a virtual private network (VPN). A VPN allows you to connect securely to another network via the Internet, preventing anyone monitoring Wi-Fi traffic from intercepting the data you send or receive.

USB charging is another source of risk. Most USB sockets allow data transfer as well as power transfer, and cyber security professionals have already demonstrated that it is possible to deliver malware and even record the screens of devices connected to chargers.[19] Mobile device and remote working policies should prohibit the use of public Wi-Fi in all but exceptional circumstances, and use USB data blockers – a USB socket with the data transfer pins removed – where public Wi-Fi is unavoidable. You might also consider disabling USB ports on laptops and other portable devices.

One vulnerability associated with remote working is one that many of us wouldn't give much thought to – eavesdropping. Most of us assume a certain degree of privacy, even in public spaces, and we discuss sensitive topics openly in bars, restaurants, etc. assuming no one is listening.

Sometimes, though, someone *is* listening. An executive who commutes via train and regularly takes business calls during the journey is a prime target for reconnaissance by hostile actors. An attacker could take the same train and sit close enough to be able to hear the executive's conversations. Given enough time, the attacker might glean useful information about the executive's organisation – information that can then be used to carry out a more technical attack. While such disclosures are naturally difficult to control, ensure that your cyber security training

---

[19] Catalin Cimpanu, "Officials warn about the dangers of using public USB charging stations", ZDNet, November 2019, *https://www.zdnet.com/article/officials-warn-about-the-dangers-of-using-public-usb-charging-stations/*.

includes advice not to discuss confidential matters in public places.

'Shoulder-surfing', where someone reads your screen over your shoulder, is another common problem when working remotely in public places. While the easiest way of mitigating this risk is simply to sit somewhere that prevents someone from viewing your screen from another angle, this isn't always an option. To add another layer of protection, provide users with privacy screens for laptops and similar devices. These reduce the effective viewing angle of the screen, making it impossible for the screen to be viewed from the side.

Example: WannaCry

In 2017, a major ransomware attack struck systems across the globe. The program, known as 'WannaCry', infected a huge number of systems across organisations including Nissan and FedEx. In the UK, the NHS was hit hard, with more than 70,000 computers and items of medical equipment affected in 80 NHS organisations. The attack saw more than 19,000 operations cancelled and cost the NHS an estimated £92 million – all because someone clicked a malicious link or opened a malicious file.

The WannaCry ransomware spread by exploiting a vulnerability in the Windows Server Message Block (SMB) protocol that allowed code to be executed on the target system. The US National Security Agency (NSA) is believed to have identified the vulnerability as far back as 2012, but instead of notifying Microsoft, it instead developed a tool to exploit the vulnerability, codenamed 'EternalBlue'.[20]

---

[20] Ellen Nakashima and Craig Timberg, "NSA officials worried about the day its potent hacking tool would get loose. Then it did.", Washington Post, May 2017,
https://www.washingtonpost.com/business/technology/nsa-officials-worried-about-the-day-its-potent-hacking-tool-would-get-loose-then-it-did/2017/05/16/50670b16-3978-11e7-a058-ddbb23c75d82_story.html.

4: Human threats

At some point – it is not clear when – the NSA realised that there was a possibility that EternalBlue had been stolen. Believing the usefulness of the tool to be diminishing and concerned for the potential impact if the exploit were to be used at scale, NSA informed Microsoft of the vulnerability. Microsoft responded quickly, releasing a critical security patch for all supported operating systems in March 2017.

In April of that year, the criminal hacker group known as the 'Shadow Brokers' released the code for EternalBlue. Two months later, WannaCry hit the headlines.

WannaCry spread as far and as fast as it did due to a combination of unclear incident response procedures and the failure to apply security patches promptly. While individual NHS organisations began informing NHS Digital, the police and others that something was wrong on the morning of the first attacks, there was no coordinated response until that evening.[21]

Microsoft's March 2017 security patch applied to all supported operating systems including Windows 7 – yet Windows 7 accounted for around 98% of WannaCry infections worldwide.[22] None of the 80 affected NHS organisations had installed the patch, despite advice to do so issued by NHS Digital in April 2017.[23]

---

[21] National Audit Office, "Investigation: WannaCry cyber attack and the NHS", April 2018, *https://www.nao.org.uk/wp-content/uploads/2017/10/Investigation-WannaCry-cyber-attack-and-the-NHS.pdf*.

[22] Russell Brandom, "Almost all WannaCry victims were running Windows 7", The Verge, May 2017, *https://www.theverge.com/2017/5/19/15665488/wannacry-windows-7-version-xp-patched-victim-statistics*.

[23] William Smart, "Lessons learned review of the WannaCry Ransomware Cyber Attack", Department of Health and Social Care, February 2018, *https://www.england.nhs.uk/wp-content/uploads/2018/02/lessons-learned-review-wannacry-ransomware-cyber-attack-cio-review.pdf*.

CHAPTER 5: PHYSICAL THREATS

Physical threats are an often-neglected aspect of cyber security, yet they can affect organisations every bit as much as technological threats. Cyber security must incorporate physical security to be truly effective – it's no good protecting sensitive data with an array of technological controls if someone can simply walk into the building and take it.

Physical security begins with identifying your perimeter and securing it, which means locks on doors and entry points to sensitive areas, like server rooms. Many organisations use keycard or PIN-entry locks to secure sensitive areas, but these carry their own risks. Staff may write down PINs to make them easier to remember, raising the risk of accidental loss or theft, while RFID proximity cards can be vulnerable to passive readers that capture the card information, allowing the attacker to create duplicates or spoof the locking mechanism with an RF emitter.

Semi-public areas like receptions and warehouses are within your perimeter, but necessarily require a different approach from something like a server room or secure area. To maintain accessibility while providing an adequate level of security, consider visitor logs, security cameras and similar techniques.

A common way for attackers to gain entry is tailgating. This is a social engineering technique used to gain access to secure buildings and areas by playing off people's innate desire to be helpful. All you need to successfully tailgate are a little preparation to ensure you don't look out of place, and the ability to think on your feet.

One tailgating tactic is for an attacker to join employees on their cigarette break pretending to be someone who recently joined the company (which conveniently explains why they don't have ID or key cards), then follow them inside when they finish. Advance reconnaissance improves the success rate of such attacks – dropping a name or two during the conversation or

5: Physical threats

mentioning a project or some other 'inside' information help reinforce the illusion that the attacker is a real employee.

Some physical entry threats are more overt. Attackers can pretend to be visiting a member of staff, or pose as a maintenance worker. Such attackers will likely refuse escorts, perhaps claiming they are running late, or that they already know the way. As soon as they are left alone, they can begin their attack, which is often used to install physical hardware such as USB keyloggers or KVM (keyboard, video, mouse) switches that allow a user to operate multiple computers from a single workstation.

Make sure your employees understand what tailgating is, and how to prevent it. Train staff to confront unfamiliar people in secure areas and ask for identification, even if the person has an apparently legitimate reason to be there. Escort visitors on the premises at all times, and ask all visitors to sign in and out to record the time spent on the premises, who they were visiting and why, etc.

Log all issued key cards and take steps to deactivate them if lost or stolen. Consider two-factor authentication (2FA), e.g. key card and PIN, and CCTV for particularly sensitive areas. Note that if CCTV covers public areas, you may have obligations under data protection legislation.

Entry threats aren't the only physical cyber security concern. Information leakage – where sensitive information is accessible to unauthorised individuals like visitors, often inadvertently – is another common physical threat.

Clear desk policies are a popular method of reducing information leakage by ensuring employees don't leave sensitive information in plain view. While useful, it is important to take a sensible, pragmatic approach to get the best results: leave sensitive paperwork in lockable drawers or filing cabinets when not in use, lock computers when away from the screen, and switch computers off overnight.

Adjacent buildings are another potential route for information leakage. Screens and even paperwork visible from adjacent

5: Physical threats

buildings are vulnerable to something as simple as a good zoom lens. Clear desk policies help with this to some extent, but don't protect you during the working day when screens and sensitive paperwork are in use. If overlooking is a concern, consider using one-way mirror film over windows to prevent people from seeing inside.

Defence in depth

Physical security doesn't stop with entry points and key-card locks. No single security measure is 100% effective, so it's important to take a defence-in-depth approach. Sometimes referred to as the 'onion skin' model of cyber security, defence in depth means having multiple, layered defences so that, if one layer fails, the other layers still protect you.

When considering your defence-in-depth options, examine your existing controls for ways they might be circumvented. Once you know where the gaps are, you can put additional 'layers' in place to take the strain should the primary control fail. Target the most likely ways your defences might be bypassed rather than assuming that everything that can go wrong will go wrong – there is little benefit in adding layers that will never be used.

As an example, consider information leakage. One major cause of information leakage is inadequate secure disposal, which you can mitigate by using the services of a certified secure disposal organisation. If that organisation somehow loses your hard-copy files or hard drives before the secure disposal process takes place, then your information is freely available to anyone who finds it.

A defence-in-depth approach would consider this possibility and take additional steps to mitigate it – for example, shredding hard-copy files or securely erasing a drive before transferring it to the disposal company. That way, if there is a failure of process during disposal, your information remains secure.

To take a defence-in-depth approach to physical security, assume that your entry defences have failed, then consider the potential vulnerabilities that may be present in your premises. Meeting rooms and common areas, for example, may contain

5: Physical threats

unsecured network ports that could allow an attacker access to your trusted network. Server rooms may be well-secured, but if positioned out of sight of foot traffic, an attacker may have enough time to bypass or defeat that security. A holistic approach will allow you to identify such risks and take steps to mitigate them.

Physical security and mobile devices

There are obvious physical security concerns for mobile devices. Encrypting phones, laptops, tablets and portable storage devices to guard against data exfiltration if the device is lost or stolen has been cyber security best practice since portable devices became mainstream. Even if the contents are encrypted, however, loss or theft of the device still amounts to loss of the data, which could be disastrous if it's not backed up elsewhere.

Defence against theft and loss may seem like common sense, but staff training to reinforce key concepts never hurts. Your mobile device policy should contain explicit requirements for the use of mobile devices: do not leave devices unattended, always store them in a secure location (e.g. a hotel safe), never store passwords with the equipment, etc.

Physical threats are often combined with social engineering and other attack types in novel ways to increase the chances that an attack will be successful. One such example is of an attacker leaving an unmarked USB device lying around where your staff are likely to spot it – perhaps in the car park, or near an entryway – in the hope that an employee sees it, picks it up, and plugs it into a computer to find out what's on it.

This attack type is surprisingly successful. A 2016 study found that 98% of USB drives left lying around a university campus were picked up, and that files were opened by the 'finder' on at least 45% of devices.[24] Such attacks play on our curiosity and

---

[24] Matthew Tischer et al, "Users really do plug in USB drives they find", Universities of Illinois and Michigan, 2016, *https://elie.net/publication/users-really-do-plug-in-usb-drives-they-find/*.

5: Physical threats

natural tendency to be altruistic (most users picked up the devices intending to return them to the owner), and can be very difficult to defend against.

USB devices can install malware or, in the worst cases, destroy the hardware of the connected PC. Devices known as 'USB killers' contain powerful capacitors that draw and store power from the USB connection. Once fully charged, the USB killer discharges the stored power back into the connected computer (or, in fact, anything with a USB port), causing irreparable hardware damage.[25]

Any unidentified mobile device found on or near the premises is a risk. Train employees to hand in found mobile devices and to understand the risks that malicious devices can pose. Regular refreshers help reinforce the message, and well-placed posters and signage are good visual reminders in the heat of the moment.

Train your IT department to test any found devices on an air-gapped, bare-bones test system so that any malware on the device cannot spread across networks, and to minimise hardware damage if the device turns out to be a USB killer.

Example: KVM attacks

Keyboard, video and mouse controllers (KVM switches, or KVMs) are devices that allow a user to switch the computer they're operating without changing keyboard, screen or mouse. KVM switches are often found in data centres, allowing operators to connect to different servers from the same workstation. KVMs from reputable manufacturers come with built-in security functions to prevent external attackers connecting to them and accessing the connected computers – but what if the KVM used to attack you belongs to someone else?

---

[25] Catalin Cimpanu, "Former student destroys 59 university computers using USB Killer device", ZDNet, April 2019, https://www.zdnet.com/article/former-student-destroys-59-university-computers-using-usb-killer-device/.

5: Physical threats

KVM attacks hit the news in 2013 with the targeting of London banks. An attacker entered a Barclays branch claiming to be IT support staff and attached a 3G-enabled KVM switch to bank computers. The 3G connection allowed the attackers to connect to the KVM through the Internet, giving them full control over the connected computer from a remote location. Once they had control, all they had to do was transfer the money from one account to another in amounts that were sufficiently small to avoid additional scrutiny.

The attackers stole £1.25 million (£600,000 of which was recovered by Barclays). A few months later, they struck another Barclays branch, resulting in the theft of £90,000. This time, the KVM switch was recovered by police, but the attackers remained at large.

In September 2013, the attackers switched targets to a Santander branch. Just as before, an attacker entered the premises under the guise of IT support staff and attached another 3G-enabled KVM device to bank computers, while accomplices were waiting to transfer funds to holding accounts. This time, however, the police were ready.

A raid carried out on an accomplice's property revealed computers in the middle of carrying out the Santander attack, along with a treasure trove of stolen credit cards, letters, usernames and passwords, and other material used to commit fraud. Police arrested the 'IT support engineer' shortly after he left the bank.[26]

The 2013 KVM attackers exploited social engineering vulnerabilities (by pretending to be IT support) to install a hardware-based threat (the 3G-enabled KVM switch). They knew enough about banking systems to ensure that the international transfers made were just below the limit that would trigger additional checks, suggesting that research and

---

[26] Tim Ring, "Cyber gang behind £1.25m 'KVM' bank fraud convicted", SC Magazine, March 2014, *https://www.scmagazineuk.com/cyber-gang-behind-125m-kvm-bank-fraud-convicted/article/1480424*.

5: Physical threats

reconnaissance was performed to identify the safest way of extracting the money without drawing attention (and likely to identify potential target branches, too).

Such 'combined' attacks are effective because they bypass many of the controls put in place to defend against them. The 3G router allowed the KVM switch to be operated over a mobile Internet connection, bypassing the bank's network security controls, while the social engineering techniques allowed the attackers to bypass physical entry controls. This is why defence in depth is so important – protecting against combined attacks requires combined defences.

CHAPTER 6: THIRD-PARTY THREATS

An increasingly interconnected world requires increasingly interconnected organisations. No matter the field your organisation operates in, there's a good chance your products or services rely on components, or even whole products produced by third parties. No doubt you also share data – via email, perhaps, or through a dedicated vendor portal. This connectivity brings great benefits, but it also exposes you to risk. You can control those risks as they relate to your organisation, but your supplier's control measures are a different story altogether.

Supply chain threats

The modern supply chain stretches across the globe and encompasses thousands of organisations. More data is shared across the supply chain than ever before, which brings increased efficiency and productivity but also introduces risk.

Once a relatively rare occurrence, attacks carried out via the supply chain have been rising steadily, with a 2019 report by Symantec noting an increase of 78% on the previous year.[27] This increase is reflected in the number of organisations that experience supply chain attacks, with a whopping 59% of respondents to a 2018 Ponemon Institute survey stating that they have experienced a data breach caused by a third party.[28]

Even if you impose extensive controls on your suppliers, attacks on your organisation through your supply chain aren't the only thing you need to consider. While many supply chain attacks are explicitly designed to exploit weaknesses in a supplier's security

---

[27] Symantec, "Internet Security Threat Report 2019", Volume 24, February 2019, *https://resource.elq.symantec.com/LP=6854*.

[28] Ponemon Institute, "Data Risk in the Third-Party Ecosystem, Third Annual Report", November 2018, *https://promotions.opus.com/l/12092/2018-11-14/6bj4g6*.

6: Third-party threats

to attack one or more of their clients, attacks intended to disrupt the supplier can still deny you access to key systems or services, often at the worst possible time.

The problem of scale

Defending against supply chain attacks is a major cyber security challenge. The first problem is one of scale. It's not uncommon for small to medium-sized organisations to have more than a hundred suppliers, and for larger organisations the numbers increase commensurately. 60% of respondents to the Ponemon Institute survey say they don't monitor third-party security or privacy practices due to a lack of resources, and this is likely just the tip of the iceberg.[29]

To overcome the problem of scale, prioritise improving supply chain security for key suppliers – those that have access to sensitive or large amounts of information and those that have the potential to cause the most disruption if an attack were to occur. Suppliers whose components are incorporated into your product or service should also be high on the list, though some of them may be able to be de-prioritised depending on the nature of your organisation – nuts, bolts and metalwork probably don't pose much of a threat, but a third-party payment processor whose service is incorporated into a web application certainly could.

Authority

Another problem is authority. Large organisations with significant buying power find it easier to impose cyber security requirements on their suppliers, but smaller organisations often struggle. 60% of respondents to the Ponemon Institute report said that suppliers refuse to allow independent monitoring or verification of their security and privacy activities, and only 23%

---

[29] Ponemon Institute, "Data Risk in the Third-Party Ecosystem, Third Annual Report", November 2018, *https://promotions.opus.com/l/12092/2018-11-14/6bj4g6*.

6: Third-party threats

conduct independent audits or third-party verification.[30] Furthermore, many organisations (47%) only conduct a legal or procurement review when considering a new supplier, yet these generally focus on the supplier's ability to meet production or service requirements and place little emphasis on cyber security.[31]

Enforcing cyber security requirements with suppliers is a thorny problem. Even in scenarios where the supplier is amenable, they may not have the resources or expertise to meet them. A pragmatic approach is essential – it is neither necessary nor practical for every supplier to employ extensive cyber security measures. Instead, tailor requirements to the supplier – consider the quantity and sensitivity of the information they have access to and how they access it, and set requirements accordingly. Remember that you have more control over your own mitigation measures than those of a supplier, so take action to reduce reliance on supplier controls by applying your own instead, where possible.

For small suppliers with only incidental access to sensitive information, a simple system like the UK's Cyber Essentials scheme might be sufficient.[32] Cyber Essentials and Cyber Essentials Plus include vulnerability scans, and the Plus scheme in particular is externally validated, providing additional confidence. Both Cyber Essentials schemes are cheap and accessible, and are ideal for smaller organisations.

Larger suppliers or those with more direct access to your information will merit more extensive requirements. You may need to plug specific gaps, such as mandating the use of 2FA when the supplier connects to your network, or you may decide

---

[30] Ponemon Institute, "Data Risk in the Third-Party Ecosystem, Third Annual Report", November 2018, *https://promotions.opus.com/l/12092/2018-11-14/6bj4g6*.

[31] Ibid.

[32] *https://www.itgovernance.co.uk/cyber-essentials-scheme*.

6: Third-party threats

to impose broader requirements, such as certification to an internationally recognised cyber security standard.

Organisations with in-house cyber security expertise should consider supporting small but critical suppliers that lack the resources or skills to manage cyber security on their own (though if you do offer support, take care to properly delineate requirements and responsibilities).

Regardless of the size of the supplier, raise cyber security as a concern up front during any contract negotiation. Ensure that contracts or agreements require the supplier to notify your organisation if they suffer a data breach or other major cyber security incident.

Understanding data flow

Perhaps the biggest problem is understanding how much data you share with your suppliers, and what they do with it after it leaves your control. However, you first need to know what data these suppliers have access to. Mapping data flows is a challenge for organisations of all sizes – even small organisations often have more data flowing in and out than they realise – but doing so is essential to grasp the full extent of the risk.

When mapping data flows, consider the whole business. Look for the points at which data enters the organisation, then follow it through each process in turn until you have a record of each processing activity and know where it is stored or transferred to at the end of the processing chain. Data flow maps must be effectively maintained in order to remain useful – it is easier and less resource-intensive to update a map when a process changes than it is to repeat the mapping exercise in its entirety every few years.

Once you know what data is shared, you can evaluate the risks posed by the way the supplier accesses the data. If the supplier has a direct connection to your network, make sure that the connection is as secure as possible and segment your network so that the supplier can only access the information they need. Employ network monitoring systems to identify any suspicious activity and keep logs to provide an evidence trail.

6: Third-party threats

With the connection between you and the supplier as secure as possible, you can then consider how the supplier processes, stores and disposes of your information. Questionnaires or on-site audits are good ways of learning what you need to know.

Ensure that any information-gathering process includes questions that will bring to light any further transfer of your data by the supplier. This seems obvious, but a striking 66% of respondents to the Ponemon Institute report don't think a supplier would tell them when sharing their data with further parties.[33] Contracts or agreements should set strict conditions on the transfer of your data by suppliers, including notification requirements.

Finally, ensure that contracts or agreements include provisions that define what happens to your information after the relationship with the supplier ends. Consider requiring proof of secure disposal or deletion for particularly sensitive data.

Cloud services

Cloud services are increasingly prevalent in modern IT operations. They offer scalable processing and storage, and can be a massive boon to organisations, yet their opacity and distance make them among the hardest systems over which to exercise effective control.

Given how difficult it can be to audit or otherwise verify the IT security of even immediate suppliers, the chances of visiting, say, Amazon's server farms to conduct a security audit are essentially zero. In many cases, you have little choice but to trust the information the Cloud provider makes available. As a result, ensuring cyber security in respect of Cloud services requires research and no small amount of trust.

---

[33] Ponemon Institute, "Data Risk in the Third-Party Ecosystem, Third Annual Report", November 2018, *https://promotions.opus.com/l/12092/2018-11-14/6bj4g6*.

6: Third-party threats

To begin securing Cloud services, canvas all areas of the business to identify all Cloud services that are in use. A 2019 study by Symantec shows that the number of Cloud services in use are often far higher than IT departments believe, so it is important to capture all of them.[34] Many services are only used on an ad hoc basis (e.g. file sharing sites for files too large to send by email), making them harder to identify.

Once all services are identified, begin information gathering. Is the provider certified to a recognised information security standard, or a member of an industry-wide scheme such as the Cloud Security Alliance? What encryption do they use? Is there provision for 2FA?

One of the most important things to understand about a potential Cloud supplier is where the data centres are located. Depending on the country in question, you may have obligations under the GDPR (or other regulations) in respect of data transfers – or you may decide that the geopolitics of the country concerned make the use of that data centre too risky.

Only allow the use of Cloud providers that meet your requirements. Consider developing an approval process and communicate this to your employees. Once you have done so, monitor use of Cloud providers across the business to see if the process is being adhered to. If it is not, you may need to block access to unapproved Cloud providers as an extra layer of defence.

Once you have selected a Cloud provider and begun using them, their security is largely out of your control. What is within your control, however, is how you and your employees use the Cloud service.

---

[34] Symantec, "Cloud Security Threat Report", Volume 1, June 2019, *https://www.symantec.com/security-center/cloud-security-threat-report*.

6: Third-party threats

Account theft and unauthorised access are responsible for 64% of Cloud security incidents, according to the 2019 Symantec report.[35] Train employees to use strong passwords and to avoid account-sharing, and regularly refresh their knowledge of phishing emails and other common threat vectors that might allow an attacker to capture login credentials. Use 2FA if the service supports it.

If the Cloud provider stores or processes sensitive information, consider using a Cloud data loss prevention (DLP) solution. These protect information sent to Cloud services by encrypting data before it is transmitted, and usually include analytics and logging tools to help identify suspicious behaviour or files.

Example: Target data breach

In 2013, US retailer Target suffered a data breach that resulted in the loss of 70 million customer records and up to 40 million payment card credentials. A successful phishing attack on one of Target's HVAC suppliers installed a Trojan that the supplier's limited cyber security measures failed to detect. The Trojan went undetected for long enough to capture the login credentials used to access Target's internal vendor portal.[36]

With those credentials, the attackers infiltrated Target's internal network and uploaded malware to several tills in Target shops, apparently to test the malware's effectiveness. Once satisfied, the attackers proceeded to upload the malware to point-of-sale (POS) devices in the majority of Target shops across the US.[37]

---

[35] Symantec, "Cloud Security Threat Report", Volume 1, June 2019, https://www.symantec.com/security-center/cloud-security-threat-report.

[36] Brian Krebs, "Target Hackers Broke in Via HVAC Company", Krebs on Security, February 2014, https://krebsonsecurity.com/2014/02/target-hackers-broke-in-via-hvac-company/.

[37] Ibid.

6: Third-party threats

Each time a customer used a card in an infected device, the malware accessed the device's memory, intercepting names, card numbers and other sensitive information. Once the information was captured, the malware encrypted it and stored it on compromised systems within Target's internal network before sending it to the attackers.

A leaked report from a penetration test carried out after the attack laid bare a number of security issues at Target, but critically, it found "no controls limiting [the tester's] access to any system, including devices within stores such as point of sale (POS) registers and servers".[38] Essentially, once the attackers had access to Target's network via the supplier's login, they had free rein to do as they pleased.

A few months later, Home Depot fell victim to a variant of the same malware.[39] 56 million payment cards and 53 million email addresses were disclosed in the attack, which – you guessed it – was traced back to a compromised supplier.[40]

The Target and Home Depot attacks shook US consumer confidence in large retailers, making clear that even huge, trusted organisations might be putting their personal information at risk. They also marked a watershed moment in the cyber security field, as organisations faced up to the risks concealed in

---

[38] Brian Krebs, "Inside Target Corp., Days After 2013 Breach", Krebs on Security, September 2015, https://krebsonsecurity.com/2015/09/inside-target-corp-days-after-2013-breach/.

[39] Brian Krebs, "Home Depot Hit By Same Malware as Target", Krebs on Security, September 2014, https://krebsonsecurity.com/2014/09/home-depot-hit-by-same-malware-as-target/.

[40] Tara Seals, "Home Depot: Massive Breach Happened Via Third-Party Vendor Credentials", Infosecurity Magazine, November 2014, https://www.infosecurity-magazine.com/news/home-depot-breach-third-party/.

6: Third-party threats

their supply chains. Incidents such as the Ticketmaster data breach in 2018, however, suggest that there is still some way to go.[41]

---

[41] Amelia Wade, "Ticketmaster data breach: Thousands of customers may be affected", Which?, June 2018, *https://www.which.co.uk/news/2018/06/ticketmaster-data-breach-thousands-of-customers-may-be-affected/*.

CHAPTER 7: SECURING THE ORGANISATION

The examples and guidance in this book are suitable for any organisation looking to improve its cyber security posture. Organisations that are taking the first steps towards cyber security, on the other hand, will quickly find that applying controls in a haphazard, reactive fashion doesn't make for a very effective system.

If your organisation is beginning its cyber security journey, a careful, planned and proactive approach provides the best results. You need to know what the risks are before you can plan how best to respond to them, and controls need to be monitored once applied to ensure they are successful. Effective cyber security cannot be implemented and forgotten about – it must be maintained and continually improved in order to be useful.

Risk management

All cyber security begins with risk management – the processes and activities an organisation uses to control risk. In turn, risk management begins with risk assessment.

Before conducting any risk assessments, develop a risk assessment process so that your results are comparable and repeatable. Without a well-defined process, you may not assess risks in a consistent manner, making it difficult to identify improvements or deficiencies as your cyber security system evolves – especially if more than one individual or team conducts assessments.

The first part of developing that process is to define your risk criteria – the limits beyond which you deem it necessary to take action – essentially your organisation's appetite for risk. This will be linked to the scales that you use to evaluate individual risks.

These scales will assess the likelihood of the risk occurring and its potential impact on the organisation. It is up to you whether

7: Securing the organisation

to use a quantitative or qualitative methodology, but subjective classifications like 'high risk' or 'low risk' need to be defined in detail or you risk their meaning shifting over time or between risk assessors, skewing later assessments.

The method doesn't need to be overly complex – in fact, simpler is generally better.

You may also wish to differentiate between asset-based risk assessments and scenario-based risk assessments. The former considers risks posed to or by specific information assets (e.g. what is the risk of someone accessing our secure database?), while the latter considers risks that arise from specific scenarios (e.g. what is the risk if the roof leaks in the server room?).

Before you can begin the risk assessment itself, you must identify your information assets. Information assets are anything that stores, interacts with or otherwise supports the use of information within the organisation. Examples include laptops, computers, servers, POS devices, mobile devices and other physical hardware, databases in electronic or hard-copy format, hard-copy filing systems, software, utility supplies (power, water, etc.) and even the premises from which you conduct business. Develop an asset register that lists the owner of the asset and where it is stored to help keep track of your assets over time.

The risk assessments should be led by someone with experience in risk management and cyber security, and should also include someone with first-hand knowledge of the asset or process in question to ensure that the risks considered are relevant and that no additional or related risks are neglected. You will also need some limited documentation: it is useful to have a form to record the assessment and the actions that arise from it in detail, and a risk register that lists all risks and associated actions to provide an at-a-glance view of the risk management process (the latter is especially helpful when reporting on your risk management process to senior executives, etc.).

With the team assembled, you can begin analysing the risk. Consider the vulnerability, the likelihood that a threat will exploit it, and the resulting impact – whether on the

7: Securing the organisation

confidentiality, integrity or availability of information, the ability to provide a service, or the business itself – and plot each against your risk acceptance criteria. If the result exceeds your risk acceptance threshold, then you need to act.

Controls

To deal with risks, we have four options: tolerate, treat, transfer and terminate.

Anything below your risk acceptance criteria will probably fall into the 'tolerate' category. This means that you accept whatever residual risk there is, but it doesn't mean that you will necessarily leave it that way – it's entirely likely that the risk will change by the next assessment, or that your organisation's risk appetite changes.

Terminating the risk means removing the source of the risk. For example, replacing an unsupported, vulnerable operating system with a newer, supported operating system. This is an effective option as it negates the risk completely, but it is often impractical – you can't always remove the source of the risk. In many cases, terminating a risk will not be possible without affecting the organisation's business objectives.

Transferring the risk means reducing it by sharing some or all of it with other parties. If the risk of operating your own data centre is too high because your office is built on a floodplain, then one way of transferring that risk would be to pay for the services of a Cloud data centre. You might also mitigate that risk by purchasing insurance, though this would arguably be a less effective way of resolving the problem – the insurance money will help you replace flood-damaged hardware, but it's not going to help you restore all your data from backups, or reduce the reputational damage caused by your service being unavailable while your systems are being restored.

In most cases, we will opt to treat a risk. To treat a risk, we apply controls that reduce the likelihood of the event, or that reduce the consequences of the event. A control might be something simple, like an annual check on a potentially leaky roof, or something more complex, like penetration testing or highly

7: Securing the organisation

segmented networks. When selecting controls, consider how easy they are to implement, the potential return on investment, and the impact on other areas of the organisation to help identify the best choice. You don't need a sledgehammer to crack a nut – simple, cheap controls can be just as effective as complex, expensive ones if they are properly used.

Broadly speaking, there are three types of control: reactive, detective and preventive. Preventive controls stop incidents from occurring (e.g. a password reset function that locks you out for a set period after several failed attempts); detective controls help you identify and understand an incident in progress (e.g. network intrusion detection); and reactive controls respond to incidents that are in progress or that have recently occurred, and mitigate negative effects, assist recovery efforts or help restore continuity, such as an incident response procedure.

Before implementing a control, you need to decide how you will monitor and maintain that control to ensure it is effective. Monitoring requires more than just an occasional glance to see if everything looks okay – to monitor, you need to measure.

When you introduce a new control, the first thing you want to know is whether it's working. To determine this, you'll need to measure performance. If you're introducing a phishing awareness training course, for example, then comparing the number of emails and other attacks reported to your support team in the three months preceding the training and the three months that follow it is one way of understanding if the control is performing as expected. This will indicate whether or not the training course is affecting the volume of reports.

Once a control is working as intended, you then measure effectiveness. This is slightly different from measuring performance: performance measurement highlights progress in implementation, whereas effectiveness measurement highlights the effect the control has on the objective you are trying to achieve.

To measure the effectiveness of the phishing awareness training, you could compare the number of reported attacks each month for the first year. If the results show that (for example) the

7: Securing the organisation

number trends downwards the further you get from the date of the training, then you might need to conduct refresher training at an appropriate point to ensure the control remains effective.

You don't need to measure every single control – focus on those that are most expensive to implement or maintain, those that mitigate the biggest risks, and those that are most likely to fail. Keep a keen eye on your other controls in the meantime and add them to your measurement plan if you think it necessary.

CHAPTER 8: INCIDENT RESPONSE AND MANAGEMENT

Perfect cyber security is an impossibility. No matter how extensive (or expensive) your defences, something will eventually get through. Large organisations are just as vulnerable as smaller organisations to zero-day vulnerabilities and attacks that take advantage of human nature – this is a big part of why large organisations with significant cyber security budgets still suffer major data breaches that hit the headlines.

The challenge, then, is how to deal with the incident when it occurs in a way that minimises disruption and allows you to get back to doing what you do best as quickly as possible. The combination of cyber security and business continuity is known as 'cyber resilience'.

To ensure you respond to an incident effectively, develop an incident response plan. In broad terms, the plan should define what constitutes an incident, who will respond to the incident, and what you will do to restore minimum operational capacity.

Defining what constitutes an incident is a key part of your plan. It is necessary to distinguish between events and incidents – put simply, an event is something that *could* affect your cyber security, but that has yet to do so, while an incident is something that *has happened* that affects your cyber security. Employees need to understand the difference so they can identify and monitor events and escalate those that turn into incidents to the response team.

Who responds to incidents is critical – your incident response team must understand the risks and issues that may arise from an incident as well as the impact on the organisation itself. It is necessary, therefore, for the team to comprise both cyber security experts and members of senior management. Specialist training may be necessary to ensure all members of the response team fully understand what is at stake during an incident.

8: Incident response and management

How you respond will vary depending on the nature of the incident in question, but there are general aspects to bear in mind when developing your plan. Major cyber security incidents are often subject to scrutiny by regulators or law enforcement authorities, so the actions you take in response should account for the need to preserve physical and electronic evidence trails in such cases, and the possibility that collection of evidence may make systems unavailable for a period of time.

In a similar vein, data breaches are often subject to mandatory reporting obligations under data protection laws, such as the EU's GDPR or Network and Information Systems (NIS) Regulations 2018. Your response plan should define how you will meet any such requirements.

Finally, develop a clear escalation path for incidents, including the level of response required. Smaller incidents may not need the involvement of the whole response team, while larger ones may require the full team and additional ad hoc participation from members of the affected business areas.

Perhaps the most important thing is to test the plan regularly to make sure that it works as intended, whether via a simple paperwork exercise, a full-scale incident simulation, or something in between. It is also important to regularly test the key components on which your response measures rely, such as data backups, independently of and at greater frequency than the testing performed on the plan itself. The failure of a key component at a critical time could imperil your whole recovery effort.

Continuity

Responding to an attack is only half the battle. The other half is getting back on your feet as quickly and efficiently as possible, with the least possible operational disruption.

Business continuity plans naturally share some space with disaster recovery plans, but the focus is different. Recovery plans focus on the technical aspects of responding to attacks, while continuity plans focus on getting the critical parts of your

8: Incident response and management

organisation – revenue streams, service functionality, etc. – back up and running so you can continue to do business.

Continuity is especially important for operators of essential services (OES) such as power and water, and for digital service providers (DSPs). The NIS Regulations, which are designed to ensure continued provision of essential and digital services in the event of a major incident, contain specific requirements in this regard. Even if you're not subject to the NIS Regulations, continuity planning can benefit your organisation – even a day or two of service disruption can result in significant financial and reputational loss.

To develop your continuity plan, conduct impact analyses on key systems, processes and service offerings to determine the extent of disruption should an incident occur. Those analyses should consider different types of disruption and their potential effects on your ability to conduct business. This will highlight recovery priorities, allowing you to better focus your efforts.

Once you know how and where to target recovery and continuity actions, you can define target recovery times for each system or service, that if exceeded would represent an unacceptable disruption. You can then consider controls and other mitigation efforts to ensure that those systems are back up and running within the target time frame.

Controls and mitigation efforts will vary depending on the type of incident. For example, many incidents will involve partial or total loss of data, so your plan should consider how and when to use backups, how to protect against cross-contamination of backups, etc. In a similar vein, many incidents involve denial of services (e.g. DDoS attacks), so your plan should consider alternative ways of providing those services, where appropriate.

As your response plan and continuity plan share much of the same ground and become active in similar circumstances, it is important to integrate the plans in a manner that complements, rather than complicates, the outcome. Where overlap exists, clearly define which plan takes priority in which circumstance to avoid competing interactions.

CHAPTER 9: STANDARDS AND FRAMEWORKS

It is perfectly possible to develop a robust cyber security system without using recognised standards or frameworks – indeed, if you've followed the guidance in this book, you're already off to a great start. As your cyber security posture evolves, however, you may find that standards or frameworks can benefit your organisation in several ways.

Standards and frameworks offer a tried, tested and comprehensive approach to cyber security developed by experts in the field. Adopting such an approach takes some of the guesswork out of developing or improving your own system, enhancing your defences in line with recognised industry best practice and accounting for aspects of cyber security that you might not otherwise have considered.

There are generally two types of standard. Some are declaratory and rely on the organisation itself to demonstrate conformity, while others allow for independent verification of conformity by an external party, but both types generally take a comprehensive approach that accounts for the wider organisation in relevant areas.

Frameworks are lists of controls and accompanying guidance, and are often more focused than standards. Frameworks are usually developed by third-sector and commercial organisations, which means that they tend to be more up to date than standards (the update process for an international standard usually takes around five years, if not longer, and requires extensive stakeholder negotiation, while third-sector and commercial organisations tend to be less restricted in this regard), but they rarely allow for independent verification.

There are standards and frameworks suitable for organisations of all sizes and all levels of cyber security experience. Some are better known in certain regions – for example, conforming to the NIST Cybersecurity Framework (CSF) might earn you plaudits

9: Standards and frameworks

in the US, but is unlikely to be familiar to UK organisations.[42] When considering standards or frameworks, choose one that is recognised in the regions in which you operate.

How far you go in applying a standard or framework is up to you. Some organisations use standards that allow for certification but forego the certification process while still applying the advice, guidance and requirements – this gives you most of the benefits of the standard without the need to pay for the certification process, or the longer-term cost of audits and other verification activities.

Certification shouldn't be dismissed lightly, however. Independently verified cyber security is the one thing that will assure current and prospective clients that you take an industry-recognised, best-practice approach to cyber security. It can also save money by allowing you to demonstrate effective cyber security in a format recognised by your clients and partners, reducing the need for them to verify it through additional audits that drain time and resources on both sides.

In many cases, adoption of standards and frameworks is driven by business need – a potential client or investor will expect a certain level of cyber security and insist that you adopt a standard or framework to prove that you can achieve and maintain it as a condition of doing business. While you can implement cyber security standards at a client's request, doing so often results in rushed development and ineffective systems. It is better to identify and adopt the most suitable standard or framework before it becomes a topic of negotiation, so you can implement it at your own pace without external pressure.

Taking the first steps

One way to approach standards and frameworks, especially if you're not sure whether they're right for your organisation, is to start small and work your way up. The UK's Cyber Essentials

---

[42] *https://www.itgovernance.co.uk/nist-cybersecurity-framework*.

9: Standards and frameworks

scheme focuses on five key cyber security controls (secure configuration, secure networks, access control, patch management and malware protection) and has two tiers of achievement: Cyber Essentials and Cyber Essentials Plus.[43]

Both tiers involve a self-assessment questionnaire and an external vulnerability scan. The 'Plus' tier requires an on-site assessment and an additional internal vulnerability scan, providing even greater assurance both for you and your clients.

If Cyber Essentials doesn't go far enough, or your clients demand that you use something that is internationally recognised, then your next stop will almost certainly be ISO 27001.[44] This international standard describes the specification for an information security management system (ISMS) – a systematic approach to managing information security risk across the whole organisation.

ISO 27001 describes 114 reference information security controls that you can apply to improve your information security (which controls are necessary is determined by risk assessment, so you only apply those that are relevant). Organisations can seek independent certification against the requirements of ISO 27001 to prove to clients and partners that they take a recognised best-practice approach to information security.

Because ISO 27001 uses the same base format as other management system standards, it can be combined with an existing management system (such as ISO 9001) to create an integrated management system. This allows you to streamline common activities such as internal audits, saving money over the long term. ISO 27001 also has a companion standard, ISO/IEC 27701, which extends the requirements of ISO 27001

---

[43] *https://www.itgovernance.co.uk/cyber-essentials-scheme*.

[44] *https://www.itgovernance.co.uk/iso27001*.

9: Standards and frameworks

to include privacy management and the security of personally identifiable information (PII).[45]

If you opt for certification against ISO 27001 and are considering an integrated management system, another excellent addition is ISO 22301, which describes a best-practice framework for business continuity management.[46] ISO 22301 strongly complements an ISMS (or any other management system) by helping you create a clear path back to business as usual after an incident, and like ISO 27001, allows for independently verified certification to provide that extra level of assurance to your clients and partners.

If you're in the US, then the NIST CSF is a good alternative to ISO 27001, though it lacks a certification pathway. The NIST CSF focuses on five 'core functions' of cyber security (identify, protect, detect, respond and recover), and has four 'implementation tiers' against which an organisation can define its current level of cyber security readiness.

---

[45] *https://www.itgovernance.co.uk/iso-27701*.

[46] *https://www.itgovernance.co.uk/iso22301-business-continuity-standard*.

CHAPTER 10: CONCLUSION

If you've made it this far, then hopefully you feel like the first steps towards cyber security are no longer an impossible climb. There are plenty of actions you can take that don't cost the earth or require extensive technological experience to implement, and if you want to take things further, there are a range of standards and frameworks that you can use to enhance and improve your programme, at the pinnacle of which are standards that offer a pathway to independent certification.

To get the best out of your cyber security programme, consider resilience and recovery alongside your cyber defence measures. A successful attack is a matter of when, not if, and a tested, effective response plan helps defend against the financial and reputational damage that follows by restoring your key revenue and support streams in a timely manner.

No matter the size of your organisation, cyber security is no longer optional – it is an essential component of business success and a critical defence against the risks of the information age. The only question left is to decide when and where your journey will begin.

FURTHER READING

IT Governance Publishing (ITGP) is the world's leading publisher for governance and compliance. Our industry-leading pocket guides, books, training resources and toolkits are written by real-world practitioners and thought leaders. They are used globally by audiences of all levels, from students to C-suite executives.

Our high-quality publications cover all IT governance, risk and compliance frameworks and are available in a range of formats. This ensures our customers can access the information they need in the way they need it.

Our other publications about cyber security include:

- *Build a Security Culture* by Kai Roer, https://www.itgovernancepublishing.co.uk/product/build-a-security-culture
- *Insider Threat – A guide to understanding, detecting, and defending against the enemy from within* by Julie Mehan, https://www.itgovernancepublishing.co.uk/product/insider-threat
- *ISO 27001 controls – A guide to implementing and auditing* by Bridget Kenyon, https://www.itgovernancepublishing.co.uk/product/iso-27001-controls-a-guide-to-implementing-and-auditing

For more information on ITGP and branded publishing services, and to view our full list of publications, visit https://www.itgovernancepublishing.co.uk/.

To receive regular updates from ITGP, including information on new publications in your area(s) of interest, sign up for our newsletter at https://www.itgovernancepublishing.co.uk/topic/newsletter.

Further reading

Branded publishing

Through our branded publishing service, you can customise ITGP publications with your company's branding.

Find out more at
https://www.itgovernancepublishing.co.uk/topic/branded-publishing-services.

Related services

ITGP is part of GRC International Group, which offers a comprehensive range of complementary products and services to help organisations meet their objectives.

For a full range of resources on cyber security visit *https://www.itgovernance.co.uk/shop/category/cyber-security*.

Training services

The IT Governance training programme is built on our extensive practical experience designing and implementing management systems based on ISO standards, best practice and regulations.

Our courses help attendees develop practical skills and comply with contractual and regulatory requirements. They also support career development via recognised qualifications.

Learn more about our training courses in cyber security and view the full course catalogue at
https://www.itgovernance.co.uk/training.

Professional services and consultancy

We are a leading global consultancy of IT governance, risk management and compliance solutions. We advise businesses around the world on their most critical issues and present cost-saving and risk-reducing solutions based on international best practice and frameworks.

We offer a wide range of delivery methods to suit all budgets, timescales and preferred project approaches.

Find out how our consultancy services can help your organisation at *https://www.itgovernance.co.uk/consulting*.

Further reading

Industry news

Want to stay up to date with the latest developments and resources in the IT governance and compliance market? Subscribe to our Weekly Round-up newsletter and we will send you mobile-friendly emails with fresh news and features about your preferred areas of interest, as well as unmissable offers and free resources to help you successfully start your projects. *https://www.itgovernance.co.uk/weekly-round-up*.

Ingram Content Group UK Ltd.
Milton Keynes UK
UKHW020932080323
418175UK00016B/1142